King Kafu and the Moon

Written by Trish Cooke

Illustrated by Andrea Castellani

Published by Pearson Education Limited, 80 Strand, London, WC2R 0RL.

www.pearsonschools.co.uk

Text © Pearson Education Limited 2016
Designed by Bigtop Design Ltd

Original illustrations © Pearson Education Limited
Illustrated by Andrea Castellani

First published in the USA by Pearson Education Inc, 2016
First published in the UK by Pearson Education Ltd, 2016

20 19 18 17 16
10 9 8 7 6 5 4 3 2

British Library Cataloguing in Publication Data
A catalogue record for this book is available from the British Library

ISBN 978 0 435 16447 8

Printed in China by Golden Cup

Contents

Chapter 1

Long ago in a far-off land, in a tiny village, there lived a king. His name was Kafu.

"I'm so brave," bragged King Kafu. "I'm not afraid of anything!"

King Kafu's people thought he was the bravest king in the world.

The thing was, King Kafu wasn't as brave as everyone thought. He had a big secret. King Kafu was afraid of the dark.

Every evening he would go to bed before it got dark. He would put on his sparkly pyjamas, then he would switch on his secret night-light and get into bed. He loved his night-light. It made the darkness in his bedroom go away, even when the sun went to bed.

One night, as usual, King Kafu went
to switch on his night-light. But the
night-light didn't come on.
"Argh!" screamed King Kafu.
He felt very afraid. King Kafu
hid under his covers as
the sun went down.

After a while, he felt
braver and he peeked
out. He saw the light from
the moon peeping through
his window. He had only ever
heard about the moon. He had
never actually *seen* it. It was so big
and bright and round!
"That's it!" he said. "The light
from the moon can keep my
bedroom bright!"

Chapter 2

A few nights later, King Kafu went to bed as usual. But when the moon rose, it looked different. A piece of the moon was missing!

The next night, King Kafu waited for the moon again. This time, even *more* of the moon was missing.

"Yaaargh!" King Kafu screamed. King Kafu's guard charged into the king's bedroom. "What is the matter?" he asked.

"The moon – it's disappearing!" cried King Kafu.

The guard looked up at the sky. He could indeed see that some of the moon was missing.

"We must save the moon!" said King
Kafu. "Tell the villagers I will give one
thousand gold coins to anyone who
can capture the moon. I will keep the
moon in the palace where I can
keep an eye on it!"

Chapter 3

The next day, the guard made the announcement to the villagers.

"The moon is disappearing!" he said. "King Kafu will give one thousand gold coins to anyone who can bring the moon to him."

The villagers were confused. The moon had disappeared before, and it had always come back again. But there was a reward of one thousand gold coins. So they started thinking of ways to capture the moon.

They decided to build a rocket.
They worked non-stop for eleven
days and nights.
    Finally, the rocket
was finished. But
when the villagers
looked up at the
sky, the moon
was gone.

"We *must* tell King Kafu," said the king's guard. He pointed to a young villager. "You, boy," he said. "Go and find the king. Tell him the moon is gone." The boy nodded and immediately set off for the palace.

Chapter 4

The boy searched the palace for the king. It took him a long time, but eventually the boy found King Kafu. He was hiding under his bed covers.

"Why are you hiding?" asked the boy.

"I'm afraid of the dark," King Kafu whimpered. "That's why I wanted to catch the moon and bring it to the palace. Then it would never be dark again. My people think I'm the bravest king in the world, but I am not. No one must ever know my secret."

The boy felt sorry for King Kafu.
"Don't worry," the boy said. "We will
find the moon and bring it to you."

The boy returned to the village. "We must find the moon's hiding place," he told the villagers.

The villagers agreed. First they collected fishing rods and butterfly nets to help them catch the moon. Then the boy, the guard, and some villagers climbed on board the rocket.

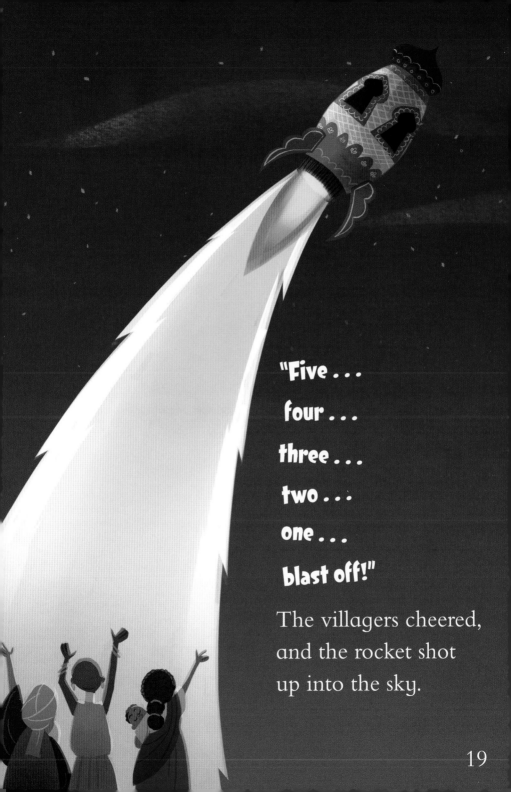

"Five . . .
four . . .
three . . .
two . . .
one . . .
blast off!"

The villagers cheered,
and the rocket shot
up into the sky.

Chapter 5

When they got into space, it was very dark. The villagers could see the moon hiding in the darkness.

"Let's fly around to the other side," said the king's guard.

"Good idea," said the boy.

The rocket zoomed around the moon, making everyone dizzy.

"Look!" said a villager, pointing out the window. "This part of the moon is bright!"

"Aha!" said the boy. "So we only see the part of the moon that the sun shines on. Let's go back and tell the king."

Back in the village, the boy went with the king's guard to the palace.

"Your Highness," said the king's guard, "there is nothing to worry about. The moon isn't disappearing at all. The moon is just dark when the sun doesn't shine on it."

"Oh dear," said King Kafu. "Whatever will we do?"